GRIMELDA
and the Spooktacular Pet Show

By Diana Murray

Illustrated by Heather Ross

KT KATHERINE TEGEN BOOKS
An Imprint of HarperCollins Publishers

HarperCollins
PUBLISHERS
Since 1817

Katherine Tegen Books is an imprint of HarperCollins Publishers.

ISBN 978-0-06-226449-7

The artist used Photoshop to create the digital illustrations for this book.
Typography by Rachel Zegar
17 18 19 20 21 SCP 10 9 8 7 6 5 4 3 2 1
❖
First Edition

For Katie B., magical editor
—D.M.

For Lobo
—H.R.

Grimelda lived in Cobweb Town,
where all the lawns were nice and brown
and every home was good and messed—
since witches liked it messed the best.

One day, Grimelda swooshed outside
to take a breezy autumn ride.
But soon she stopped her broom to see
a flyer posted on a tree.

SPOOKTACULAR
PET SHOW

A contest for pets,
spooktacular pets . . .

Who'll be the winner?
It's anyone's guess.

*Note: For your safety, please
follow all codes.
**Warning: Some losers may
turn into toads.

She flew straight home and parked her broom,
then searched her very messy room.

She found a trail of muddy tracks,

an empty bag of Batnip Snacks,

a mixed-up pile of socks and shorts—
and underneath was Wizzlewarts.

You cozy ball of thistle fluff! Are you spooktacular enough?

Just then her neighbor Hildegard
went flying by above the yard.
Her dragon, Blaze, was bold and strong.
His tail alone was ten feet long!

While Blaze breathed fire and fiercely roared . . .
Wizzlewarts curled up and snored.
He lay there like a powder puff.

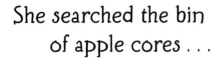

behind the couch,
and under rugs . . .

and in her pail of
slimy slugs.

She swept her mess from here to there.
That spell book wasn't anywhere.

Grimelda paced. She rubbed her chin.

No spell means
Wizzlewarts
can't win.

She grabbed her broom; her mind was set.
She'd have to get a better pet.

She flew to Zelda's General Store
and found one hairy mountain boar,
who snorted with his tiny snout.
(The other pets were all sold out.)

Grimelda bought some Batnip Snacks,
an eye-scream cone, and broomstick wax.
But not that shaggy heap of fur.

She searched both near . . . and far away.
It took all night and half the day.

Too cute.

Too pink.

Too plain.

Too small.

They're not spooktacular at all!

Her wand became a rod and reel,
and soon she caught a *monster* eel.
With spiky fins and huge fangs, too,
this pet seemed like a dream come true!

But then it growled and swished its tail.
"Uh-oh." Grimelda's face turned pale.
The monster slithered after her.

A little *too* spooktacular!

She flew back home

and slammed the door
(she'd never flown that fast before),

then sighed and slumped down in her seat,
prepared to just accept defeat . . .

. . . when something glowed beneath the bed.
She bent down low. "What's that?" she said.

And there, beside her dusty hat,
was Wizzlewarts . . . that clever cat!

He'd found her spell book! And what's more,
he'd flipped to page three hundred four—

The Perfect Spell
to Make a Cat
Spooktacular
in Seconds Flat!

Just then the clock began to chime.
With luck they'd make it just in time.
"Can't stop to practice now," she said.
She grabbed her broom and off they sped.

A big crowd gathered at the show,
where pets were lined up in a row—
from pets with spikes and pets with scales
to frogs and hogs and haunted snails.

BACKSTAGE

SPOOK-tacular PET SHOW TODAY!

And one by one, they each performed.
They stomped and growled, did tricks, transformed!

Grimelda watched Blaze blow his flame
and then she gulped. They'd called her name!
She grabbed her cat and smoothed her dress.
(That eye-scream sure had made a mess!)

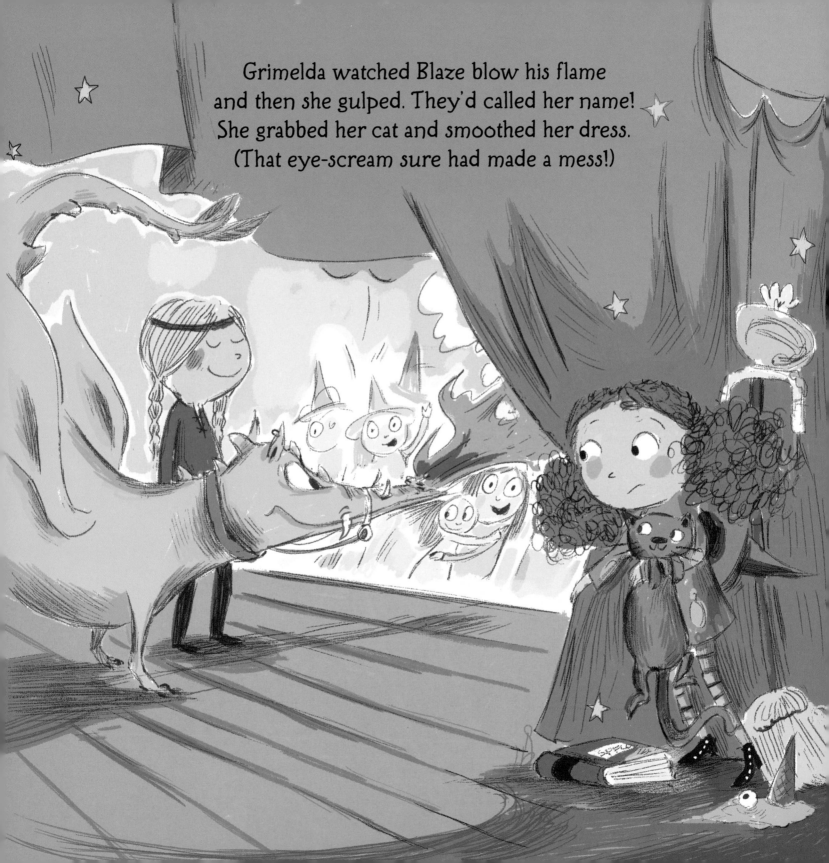

She found the spell. "Ah yes, right here!"
But then her finger left a smear.
Was that a blob of eye-scream fudge?
Oh no! She'd made a bigger smudge!

Her knees turned weak as mudworm jelly.
Bat wings fluttered in her belly.
Now the page was blotched and blurred!
She squinted hard to see each word.

But still she held her wand out strong.
"Oh, please, don't let my spell go wrong!"

A cloud of glitter burst—

Oh no! Her cat was *cuter* now!

The speechless judges blinked their eyes.
Then came another big surprise,
for as Grimelda wiped the page . . .

. . . that monster eel squirmed up onstage!
It leaped at her with snapping jaws,
but Wizzlewarts . . .

. . . showed off his claws!

He yowled and arched
his back and hissed.

The eel spat balls of slime
but missed!

She bravely aimed her wand and then
she yelled her messed-up spell again:

Huffery-puffery, winkety-wink,
poofety-moofety! Pinkety-PINK!

A cloud of glitter burst—

KAPOW!

Grimelda laughed and took a bow.

The judges cheered! The crowd went wild!
Grimelda hugged her cat and smiled.

The curtain closed. The show was done.

We did it,
Wizzlewarts!
We won!

Their prizes were: a pouch of gold,
a trophy, and a jar of mold,
a year's supply of broomstick wax . . .

. . . and fifty bags of Batnip Snacks.